YOU *can* SPEAK KOREAN

YOU *can* SPEAK KOREAN

by
Choonwon Kang

HOLLYM

About the Author

CHOONWON KANG was born in Korea, and studied in English Language and Literature at Ewha Womans University (B.A.). She later obtained her M.A. degree in English Linguistics from George Mason University, Fairfax, Virginia, and received a Ph.D. in Linguistics from Georgetown University, Washington, D.C. For many years she has engaged herself in teaching profession, and at present she is a Guest Professor of English at Kyungnam University, Masan, Korea.

Author's Acknowledgments

I would like to thank:

Chairman Rhimm Insoo of Hollym Corporation, who believed in me from the start and who still does after almost 10 years (I am so glad I can get him this book before 10 years is up), who is the only person I can not prove myself for punctuality I am known for with people around me;

President Chu Shin-won and his staff at Hollym, especially Ms. Uhm Kyoung-hee and Miss Kang Sue-jung, for their patience and hard work;

Dr. Kim Jewan at Seoul National University, who bridged me with Hollym Corporation ;

Prof. Lee Yong-woong at Kyungnam University who brushed up on my Korean of 15 years' absence ;

And all the students, who have taken my course at Johns Hopkins University, at Chinhae(University of Maryland), and at Korean Schools in the Metropolitan Washington area, for their questions and comments.

First published in 1994
Third Impression, 1995
by Hollym International Corp.
18 Donald place, Elizabeth, New Jersey 07208 U.S.A.
Phone:908)353-1655 Fax:(908)353-0225

Published simultaneously in Korea
by Hollym Corporation; Publishers
14-5 Kwanchol-dong, Chongno-gu, Seoul 110-111 Korea
Phone:(02)735-7551~4 Fax:(02)730-5149

ISBN:1-56591-020-6
Library of Congress Catalog Card Number:94-75557

Illustrations by Bae Su-kyung and Kim Hung-in

Printed in Korea

To

my parents

Seong Ho and Haesoon Kang

who

made me Korean

(made in Korea)

TABLE OF CONTENTS

PREFACE

You Can Speak Korean is designed for people who need the survival skills in Korean at the beginning level. This book can be used as a textbook of Korean at the college level or a must-read guide in language and culture for tourists to Korea.

This book is divided into four chapters:
1. Han'gŭl, the Korean Alphabet, which explains how to match symbols and sounds;
2. Elements of the Korean Language, which explains minimal grammar necessary for elementary proficiency and deals with things uniquely Korean;
3. Useful Expressions, which focuses on speaking and listening skills in various situations; and
4. Reading, which introduces Korean customs by short reading passages adequate for beginners of Korean.

Depending on the need of the users, one or more chapters can be selected for learning or for a quick reference. If you are in desperate need to master the Korean alphabet in a very short time, say, a tourist who needs to read the road signs or a businessman who needs to get around the city, consult the first chapter. If you depend heavily on grammar as the basis of language proficiency, select a page or two on the topic at hand in the second chapter. If you need to deal with Korean people and wish to speak at least a few phrases, find the situation in the third chapter and practice. Working with the tape will be very useful at this point. If you have little knowledge of Korea, scan the fourth chapter as a brief orientation to Korea. If you are pressed for time, you can read the translations given for the written texts.

You Can Speak Korean is easy in every attempt.

First, it is not thick, but slim. Since it is manageable in size and volume, it is easy-to-master. If you do not have a chunk of time, use it whenever necessary and keep it as a reference. I will be happy to find this book in your car, in the hotel room, in your briefcase, on the kitchen table, or in the bathroom.

Second, looking up is made easy. From the table of contents, the English-Korean glossary, to the list of vocabulary, you can save time by cross-checking.

Third, the Korean alphabet is introduced in a new order. It is organized in such a step-by-step fashion that it is easy-to-learn.

Fourth, the particular situation you are in is easy-to-find among real life situations. If it is not the same situation, I hope you will find the closest one similar to what you are looking for and apply your analytic ability for a try.

In order to achieve our ultimate goal of communication either active or passive, the following schemes are employed.

Practice

The focus is threefold: practice pronouncing (mimicking native speakers) in chapter one; practice speaking and practice listening in chapter three. When you are engaged in a conversation, you may be either at the receiving end or at the producing end.
There are receptive phrases that you listen and understand, for example, you are asked to fill out a registration form when you check into a hotel, and there are productive phrases that you say in order to get your meaning across or to get things done, for example, when you order food at a restaurant. At the early stage of learning a new language, it is better to have the number of new phrases at a minimum. This way the attack on an unfamiliar language will be made easy. If a situation requires receptive skills, focus on listening; if another situation requires productive skills, focus on speaking.

In addition to practice, there are exercises and questions which test your grasp of the topic being discussed. Answers are provided for you in an upside down fashion.

Notes

Throughout the book the notes are presented to help you understand the text better. These notes include both grammatical and cultural ones.

Dialog

Since the goal of this book is to provide practical conversational phrases with minimal grammar and cultural notes, the phrases were taken from everyday casual conversation occurring naturally, very often without particles. Therefore, the dialogs presented here are the ones you will hear most likely in a given situation and the ones you will say most likely. Try and see how it works. It took me a long time to realize that anything longer than one syllable to a non-native speaker of Korean is as much harder as the number of extra syllables beyond one. Here is the selectional principle of simplicity: As long as I can find shorter and simpler phrases to achieve the goal of communication, those were selected. I will be happy if you master at least one phrase from each lesson. Am I asking too much? Let me know how you are doing.
Good luck!

VOWELS

Symbols	Approximates	Examples	
ㅏ	<u>ah</u>	아이	*child*
ㅐ	b<u>ay</u>	애인	*lover*
ㅑ	<u>ya</u>rd	야구	*baseball*
ㅒ	<u>ya</u>nk	애기	*story*
ㅓ	<u>u</u>nder	언니	*female sibling*
ㅔ	<u>e</u>ngine	엔진	*engine*
ㅕ	<u>you</u>ng	여자	*female*
ㅖ	<u>ye</u>s	예수	*Jesus*
ㅗ	— (<u>eau</u> in French)	오이	*cucumber*
ㅘ	<u>wa</u>tt	왕	*king*
ㅙ	<u>wa</u>it	왜	*why*
ㅚ	— (p<u>eu</u> in French)	외국	*foreign country*
ㅛ	<u>yo</u>yo	요리	*cooking*
ㅜ	<u>oo</u>ps	우유	*milk*
ㅝ	<u>wo</u>nderful	원숭이	*monkey*
ㅞ	<u>We</u>ndy	웬	*what kind of*
ㅟ	<u>we</u>	위	*up*
ㅠ	<u>you</u>	유리	*glass*
ㅡ	—	으뜸	*number one*
ㅢ	—	의사	*doctor*
ㅣ	<u>ee</u>l	이유	*reason*

CONSONANTS

Symbols	Approximates	Examples	
ㄱ	good	구	nine
ㄴ	nun	너	you
ㄷ	dog	도구	tool
ㄹ	radio	라디오	radio
ㅁ	moon	문	door
ㅂ	Bob	밥	cooked rice
ㅅ	spring	소	cow
ㅇ	no value	이	teeth
ㅈ	judge	자	ruler
ㅊ	choice	초	candle
ㅋ	key	키	height
ㅌ	tell	테	frame
ㅍ	pea	피	blood
ㅎ	ham	해	sun
ㄲ	skill	토끼	rabbit
ㄸ	still	띠	band
ㅃ	spill	삐다	to sprain
ㅆ	sill	쌀	rice
ㅉ	cats	짜다	to wring

HAN'GŬL, THE KOREAN ALPHABET

1.1   BASIC VOWELS AND BASIC CONSONANTS

1.1.1   ㅏ   ㅣ   ㅜ

Vowels	Approximates
ㅏ	<u>ah</u>
ㅣ	<u>ee</u>l
ㅜ	<u>oo</u>ps

1) ㅏ ··· The position of the tongue is at the lowest. The shape of the mouth is wide and open. The sound is coming from the midway between the front and the back of the mouth.
2) ㅣ ··· The tongue is in high position. The sound is coming from the front of the mouth.
3) ㅜ ··· This is coming from the back of the mouth. The lips are rounded.

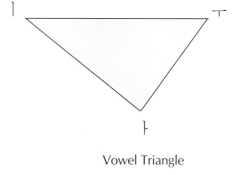

Vowel Triangle

1.1.2   ㅓ   ㅗ   ㅡ

Vowels	Approximates
ㅓ	<u>u</u>nder
ㅗ	[<u>ow</u>] for the letter 'o'
ㅡ	unrounded ㅜ

1) ㅓ ··· ㅓ is higher than ㅏ in the position of the tongue. The lip shape of ㅓ is smaller than that of ㅏ.
2) ㅗ ··· The tongue position is lower than that of ㅜ.

The shape of the lips is round.

The closest approximate is the beginning sound of the English letter 'o' :short and blunt, as in *eau* in French.

3) ㅡ ⋯ This is an unrounded version of ㅜ: It is coming from the place almost the same as that of ㅜ, but lips are not rounded.

There is no equivalent in English.

The pronunciation of the following four vowels can be indicated in relative terms. The first column shows how open the mouth is; The second column shows the distance between the top of the tongue and the roof of the mouth; The third column shows if the tongue is extended forward or retracted.

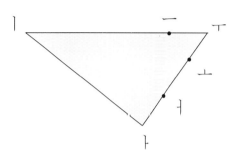

Vowel Triangle

	Openness of the Mouth	Height of the Tongue	Tongue Extension/Retraction
ㅏ	more open	lower	more front
ㅓ	↕	↕	↕
ㅗ			
ㅜ	more closed	higher	more back

Practice

아이

아우

오이

child   younger brother   cucumber

NOTES

1 Symbol 'ㅇ' as in 아 is a consonant, but it has no sound as an initial element in a syllable. See 1.1.4 for detail.

2 Each syllable has to be pronounced separately with equal stress.

1.1.3 ㅑ ㅕ ㅛ ㅠ

These four vowels are diphthongs, which begin with one sound and end with another sound. For example, when you pronounce ㅑ, you begin with ㅣ and end with ㅏ. Each diphthong here begins with 'ㅣ', which is not a full-fledged vowel, but a semivowel. This is also called a glide because it only stays for a very short time and quickly moves to a more lingering sound. Say ㅑ for five minutes and what you will hear at the end is a simple vowel ㅏ.

		Begin		End	Approximates
ㅑ	=	ㅣ	+	ㅏ	yard
ㅕ	=	ㅣ	+	ㅓ	young
ㅛ	=	ㅣ	+	ㅗ	yoyo
ㅠ	=	ㅣ	+	ㅜ	you

Practice

여우   우유

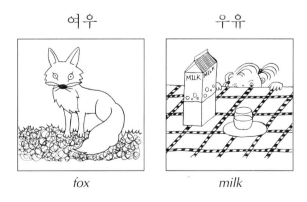

fox   milk

1.1.4 ㅇ

(The sound value of each consonant in 1.1 and 1.2 is based on the word-initial use.)

When this consonant ㅇ is placed initially in a syllable, as in 아이, it does not have any sound value ; it simply functions as a place holder. This means that 아이 is pronounced as if there were two vowels, namely, ㅏ and ㅣ .

1.1.5 ㅁ   ㄴ

Both sounds are produced through the nose because the passage through the mouth is blocked.

Consonants	Approximates		
ㅁ	<u>m</u>oon	무	The upper and lower lips touch.
ㄴ	<u>n</u>un	누	The tip of the tongue touches just behind the tooth ridge.

Practice

나	너	무	누나
I	*you*	*radish*	*a boy's older sister*

나무	이마	어머니	아니오
tree	*forehead*	*mother*	*no*

1.1.6 ㄹ

Consonant	Approximate	
ㄹ	radio	라디오

Pure Korean has no word-initial ㄹ's. That is, the words that start with ㄹ are mostly borrowed ones from foreign languages, having the value of an [r], as in 'radio' and 'robot'.

Practice

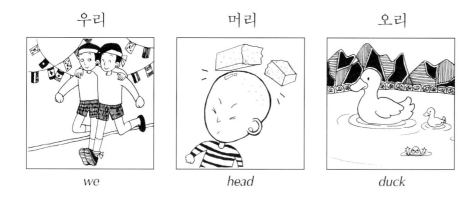

우리   머리   오리

we   *head*   *duck*

1.1.7 ㅂ   ㄷ   ㅈ   ㄱ

These four consonants are made by a complete blockage of the airstream at some point in the vocal tract.

Consonants	Approximates		
ㅂ	Bob	비	The lips are completely closed.
ㄷ	dog	도구	Closure is made between the gum region and the teeth.
ㅈ	judge	자	Closure is made behind the gum.
ㄱ	good	가구	Closure is made at the root of the tongue.

Practice

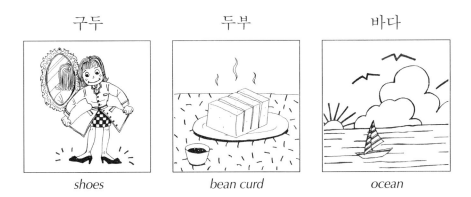

구두   두부   바다

shoes   *bean curd*   *ocean*

1.1.8 ㅅ

Consonant	Approximate		
ㅅ	<u>s</u>pring	소	Friction is made between the gum and the teeth.

Practice

수저   사자   저수지

a spoon and chopsticks   *lion*   *reservoir*

1.1.9 ㅍ ㅌ ㅊ ㅋ

The common property of these four is aspiration, which involves the puff of air coming from the mouth. These aspirated sounds have their plain counterparts: ㅂ, ㄷ, ㅈ, ㄱ.

Consonants	Approximates	
ㅍ	pea	피
ㅌ	tea	티
ㅊ	choice	초
ㅋ	key	키

Plain   : ㅂ ㄷ ㅈ ㄱ
Aspirated : ㅍ ㅌ ㅊ ㅋ

The symbols in each set are similar. The difference is that the aspirated counterpart has one more stroke.

Practice

차　　　　　파　　　　　코　　　　토마토

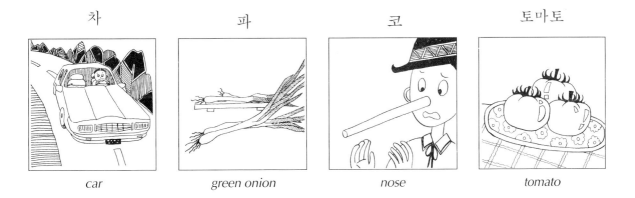

car　　　　　green onion　　　　nose　　　　　tomato

1.1.10 ㅎ

Consonant	Approximate		This is another aspirated sound , but without much harshness.
ㅎ	<u>h</u>ouse	하루	

Practice

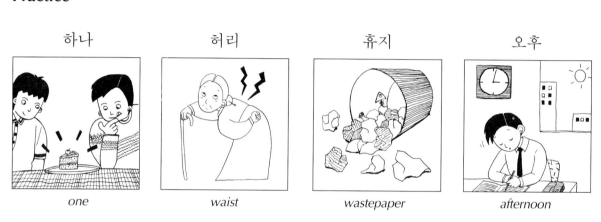

하나   허리   휴지   오후

one   *waist*   *wastepaper*   *afternoon*

Review Practice

여보	소녀	바지
여자	어서	이유
이사	아버지	구조
부모	다리	서로
모자	교수	바구니
주머니	거리	우주
나무	사고	

1.2 MORE VOWELS AND MORE CONSONANTS

1.2.1 ㅔ ㅐ

ㅔ   b<u>e</u>d   베
ㅐ   b<u>a</u>y   배

As you go down the vowel triangle, the mouth gets more open and the position of the tongue gets lower. Therefore, ㅐ is more open than ㅔ.

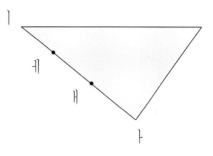

Vowel Triangle

Practice

개 — dog

게 — crab

해 — sun

아래 — below

애기 — baby

세배 — New Year's bow

노래 — song

배구 — volleyball

1.2.2 ㅖ ㅒ

	Begin		End		
ㅖ	=	ㅣ	+	ㅔ	yes	예수
ㅒ	=	ㅣ	+	ㅐ	yank	애기

While ㅔ and ㅐ are simple sounds, ㅖ and ㅒ are diphthongs.

Practice

시계   세계   차례

watch   world   turn

1.2.3 ㅘ ㅙ ㅚ

ㅘ	=	ㅗ	+	ㅏ	watt	사과
ㅙ	=	ㅗ	+	ㅐ	wait	왜
ㅚ	=	ㅗ	+	ㅣ	almost same as ㅙ	외조

NOTES

1 The first part of the combination is a semivowel, which involves the rounding of the lips.

2 ㅚ is pronounced either as a simple vowel (as in French *peu*) or as a diphthong (closer to the combination of ㅗ + ㅐ). Due to the extra effort required to pronounce it as a simple vowel, people tend to pronounce it as a diphthong, thus resulting in no difference between ㅚ and ㅙ.

Practice

과자 confectioncry

돼지 pig

좌우 left and right

회사 compuny

1.2.4 ㅝ ㅞ ㅟ

ㅝ	= ㅜ + ㅓ	<u>wa</u>nt	뭐
ㅞ	= ㅜ + ㅔ	<u>We</u>ndy	웬
ㅟ	= ㅜ + ㅣ	<u>we</u>	위

The first part in the combination, ㅜ, is a semivowel. The only difference between the semivowels ㅗ and ㅜ, is the degree of clearness of its sound : clear ㅗ vs. dark ㅜ.

Practice

귀 ear

쥐 rat

쉬다 to rest

추위 cold weather

1.2.5 ㅢ

	Begin	End	
ㅢ =	ㅡ	+ ㅣ	의미

There is no equivalent for this in English. Even though it is a diphthong (which starts with ㅡ and ends with ㅣ), a lot of people pronounce it as a simple vowel, either ㅡ or ㅣ, depending on the dialects.

Practice

의자   의회   의사   회의

chair   parliament   doctor   meeting

1.2.6 ㄲ ㄸ ㅃ ㅆ ㅉ

These five consonants are double in formation and tense in pronunciation. There are single counterparts respectively : ㄱ, ㄷ, ㅂ, ㅅ, ㅈ. Double consonants require more muscle tension than single ones.

1.3   ORDER AND POSITIONING OF VOWELS

1.3.1 Order of Vowels

So far the vowels have been introduced from simple to complex ones for your convenience. However, there is a definite order among them, which one needs to know in order to look up a dictionary.

1.3.1.1 Basic 10

ㅏ   ㅑ   ㅓ   ㅕ   ㅗ   ㅛ ㅜ   ㅠ ㅡ   ㅣ

1.3.1.2 All 21 (Basic 10 and 11 More)

Easy-to-read layers

ㅏ ㅐ ㅑ ㅒ

ㅓ ㅔ ㅕ ㅖ

ㅗ ㅘ ㅙ ㅚ ㅛ

ㅜ ㅝ ㅞ ㅟ ㅠ

ㅡ ㅢ ㅣ

1.3.2 Positioning of Vowels

Korean vowels need to be positioned in the right place in relation to initial consonants. They will look un-Korean otherwise.

1.3.2.1 Vowels Positioned to the Right of Consonants (CV)

ㅏ ㅐ ㅑ ㅒ ㅓ ㅔ ㅕ ㅖ ㅣ

(가 개 갸 걔 거 게 겨 계 기)

1.3.2.2 Vowels Positioned to the Bottom of Consonants ($\frac{C}{V}$)

ㅗ ㅛ ㅜ ㅠ ㅡ

(고 교 구 규 그)

1.3.2.3 Combined Vowels ($C\!\!\!/\!\!\sqrt{}$)

ㅘ ㅙ ㅚ ㅝ ㅞ ㅟ ㅢ

(과 괘 괴 궈 궤 귀 긔)

1.4 CONSONANTS AS FINAL ELEMENTS(*PACH'IM*)

Consonants can be placed initially or finally in a syllable, for example, ㅎ and ㄴ in 한. All 19 consonants can be used initially, but only 16 consonants (except ㄸ, ㅃ, ㅉ) can appear finally. The consonant used as a final element in a syllable is called 'pach'im' (받침). For some consonants there is a slight change in its sound value between the initial element and the final element. The number of sound value available as pach'im is only seven : ㅇ, ㅁ, ㄴ, ㄹ, ㅂ, ㄷ,

1.4.1 ㅇ

Unlike the initial ㅇ as a place holder, the final ㅇ has a definite value 〔 ŋ 〕 as in <u>sing</u>.

Practice

공	방	왕	강
ball	*room*	*king*	*river*

종	병	콩	땅
bell	*bottle*	*bean*	*earth*

1.4.2 ㅁ ㄴ

The sound value of these two consonants as final elements remain the same as initial elements.

Practice

눈
snow/eye

돈
money

손
hand

산
mountain

봄
spring

곰
bear

밤
night/chestnut

힘
strength

1.4.3 ㄹ

The syllable-final ㄹ's are pronounced like an [l] as in bil<u>l</u>.

Practice

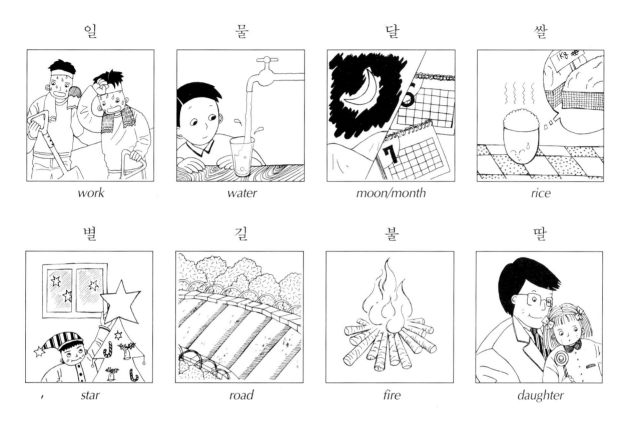

일 — work

물 — water

달 — moon/month

쌀 — rice

별 — star

길 — road

불 — fire

딸 — daughter

1.4.4   ㅂ   ㄷ   ㄱ

The sound value of an initial ㅂ is the same as a final ㅂ except for releasing, as in 밥. Do not release the final consonants when you pronounce them. When you do, they sound un-Korean.

The three consonants (ㅂ, ㄷ, and ㄱ) can be considered representatives of each set, which is shown next page. This means that the consonants in each set sound the same when they are placed as final elements in a syllable. Thus, 입 and 잎 sound exactly the same.

ㅂ	ㄷ	ㄱ
ㅍ	ㅅ	ㅋ
	ㅈ	ㄲ
	ㅊ	
	ㅌ	
	ㅎ	
	ㅆ	

Practice

집   앞   빗   빛

house   *front*   *comb*   *light*

밭   옷   목   부엌

field   *clothes*   *neck*   *kitchen*

Review Practice

공항

airport

우산

umbrella

할머니

grandmother

한국

Korea

가을

autumn

버섯

mushroom

꽃

flower

바늘

needle

한글

Korean alphabet

반지

ring

1.5 NAMES OF CONSONANTS

Now that you know how to pronounce all the vowels and consonants in the Korean alphabet, it is time to learn the name of each consonant.

1.5.1 Regulars

The name of a single consonant consists of two syllables. Suppose we name ㄴ. The first syllable consists of the consonant being discussed ㄴ and the vowel ㅣ, and the second syllable consists of ㅇ, the vowel ㅡ, and the same consonant ㄴ, thus 니은. Try the following :

ㄴ	ㄹ	ㅁ	ㅂ	ㅇ	ㅈ	ㅊ	ㅋ	ㅌ	ㅍ	ㅎ
니은	리을	미음	비읍	이응	지읒	치읓	키읔	티읕	피읖	히읗

1.5.2 Irregulars

ㄱ	ㄷ	ㅅ
기역	디귿	시옷

There are three consonants which do not conform to the rule above.

1.5.3 Double Consonants

There are five double consonants : ㄲ, ㄸ, ㅃ, ㅆ, ㅉ. Since these are formed by doubling their single counterparts, they are named by adding the word 쌍 (meaning 'double') in front.

ㄲ	ㄸ	ㅃ	ㅆ	ㅉ
쌍기역	쌍디귿	쌍비읍	쌍시옷	쌍지읒

1.6 SYMMETRIC CONSONANTS

Plain(Lax)	:	ㄱ	ㄷ	ㅂ	ㅅ	ㅈ
Aspirated	:	ㅋ	ㅌ	ㅍ		ㅊ
Tense	:	ㄲ	ㄸ	ㅃ	ㅆ	ㅉ

In order to understand the Korean consonantal system, another summary will be useful : The consonants in each column, such as ㅂ, ㅍ, ㅃ, have the same place of articulation (two lips are involved in this case). However, the manners are different: Aspirated ones (ㅋ, ㅌ, ㅍ, ㅊ) add aspiration, which is realized as the puff of air from the mouth, while tense ones (ㄲ, ㄸ, ㅃ, ㅆ, ㅉ) add more muscle tension than the plain ones (see 1.1.9 and 1.2.6 for detail).

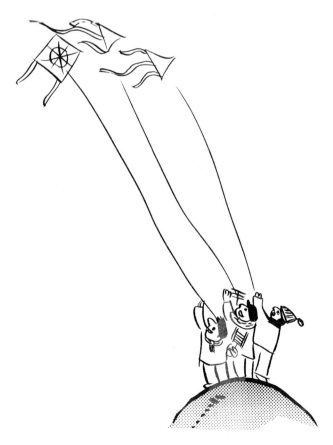

1.7 *PACH'IM* AS COMBINED CONSONANTS

ㄱ	ㄴ	ㄹ	ㅂ	ㅅ
ㄲ	ㄴㅈ	ㄹㄱ	ㅂㅅ	ㅆ
ㄱㅅ	ㄴㅎ	ㄹㅁ		
		ㄹㅂ		
		ㄹㅅ		
		ㄹㅌ		
		ㄹㅍ		
		ㄹㅎ		

The Korean consonantal system may look very complicated with these combined consonants, but there are only a few that are used frequently. The ones with high frequency are 앉다, 않다, 읽다, 없다, 있다. Since one can not pronounce two consonants at the same time, one of the combination is represented as a final sound. There is no set rule for this selection. However, when one is selected, sometimes the other affects the value of a following consonant. Take 않다 for example. ㄴ is chosen to represent the sound of pach'im, but ㅎ adds aspiration to the following consonant ㄷ, which makes 않다 pronounced as 안타.

1·8 RULES OF PRONUNCIATION

1.8.1 Liaison

When a syllable-final consonant is followed by a vowel, the consonant is carried over to the next syllable as if it were the initial element. For example, 집에 is pronounced as 지베.

Practice

국이	옷이
문이	꽃을
달이	잎이
이름이	밖에
밥을	있어

In case you have combined consonants as the final element, such as ㄹㅁ in 젊은, you still apply liaison : Leave the first one ㄹ behind and carry the second one ㅁ to the next syllable, thus 절믄.

Practice

앉아	핥아
긁어	흙을
밟아서	읊어
삶을	없어요
밝으면	읽어

1.8.2 Nasalization

감사합니다 → 감사함니다

ㅂ takes on the nasal feature of the immediately following consonant ㄴ and changes to ㅁ (ㅂ + ㄴ → ㅁ, ㄴ),which is closer to ㅂ in nature by having a nasal feature and having the same place of articulation (ㅂ and ㅁ are produced at the same place). Sometimes a consonant changes into the same sound as in 입맛 → 임맛(ㅂ + ㅁ → ㅁ, ㅁ). The following chart shows what nasal feature the plain consonants take on depending upon the place of articulation.

(Nasals)	ㅁ	ㄴ	ㅇ
	↑	↑	↑
(Plains)	ㅂ	ㄷ	ㄱ
	ㅍ	ㅌ	ㅋ
		ㅅ	
		ㅆ	
		ㅈ	
		ㅊ	
		ㅎ	

공부합니다 → 공부함니다
낱말 → 난말
학년 → 항년

Practice

국물   숙녀
앞머리   작문
부엌문   꽃나무
듣는다   돕는다
한국말   안녕하십니까

1.8.3 Aspiration

When any of the consonants in a set (ㄱ, ㄷ, ㅂ, ㅈ) is placed before or after ㅎ, each changes into its aspirated counterpart (ㅋ, ㅌ, ㅍ, ㅊ), which is considered to have assimilated into the aspirated feature of ㅎ : ㄱ+ㅎ → ㅋ or ㅎ+ㄱ → ㅋ.

ㄱ → ㅋ	생각하다 → 생가카다
ㄷ → ㅌ	노랗다 → 노라타
ㅂ → ㅍ	입히다 → 이피다
ㅈ → ㅊ	많지 → 만치

Practice

졸업하다	익히기
빨갛다	긁히다
옳지	놓다
많고	좋군
시작하다	않다

1.8.4 Tensing

Lax or plain consonants (ㄱ, ㄷ, ㅂ, ㅅ, ㅈ) become tense (ㄲ, ㄸ, ㅃ, ㅆ, ㅉ).

1) When a voiceless consonant (ㄱ, ㄷ, ㅂ, ㅅ, ㅈ) is preceded by another voiceless consonant :

ㄱ → ㄲ	학교 → 학꾜
ㄷ → ㄸ	식당 → 식땅
ㅂ → ㅃ	국밥 → 국빱
ㅅ → ㅆ	학생 → 학쌩
ㅈ → ㅉ	숙제 → 숙쩨

강 # 가	→	강까
발 # 등	→	발뜽
산 # 불	→	산뿔
눈 # 사람	→	눈싸람
밤 # 잠	→	밤짬

# indicates a word boundary

2) In combined nouns, when a word-initial voiceless consonant is preceded by a word-final voiced consonant (ㄴ, ㄹ, ㅁ, ㅇ).

Practice

선달

적자

잡담

걷기

산길

달밤

벌집

돌덩이

December   *deficit*   *chat*   *walking*

mountain trail   *moonlit night*   *beehive*   *stone*

1.8.5 Palatalization

ㄷ → ㅈ   미닫이 → 미다지
ㅌ → ㅊ   같이 → 가치

A consonant (ㄷ, ㅌ) takes on the palatal feature of the following vowel ㅣ and changes into its palatal counterpart (ㅈ, ㅊ).

Review Practice

감사합니다

thank you

손짓

gestures

먹는다

to eat

낮에

daytime

식사

meal

떡국

rice-cake soup

파랗다

being blue

작년

last year

끝으로

at the end

찾는다

to search

ELEMENTS OF
THE KOREAN LANGUAGE

2

2.1 STYLES OF SPEECH

Korean utilizes different styles of speech, which vary from one situation to another. Some determining factors which contribute to this variety are the social status, age, sex, relationship between the speakers, and the formality of the situation.

There are at least four styles of speech :

1 The Polite-formal Style   : 안녕히 가십시오.
2 The Polite-informal Style : 안녕히 가세요.
3 The Plain-informal Style   : 잘   가요.
4 The Plain Style   : 잘   가.

NOTES

1 The words 안녕히 and 잘 express the same thing, an adverbs meaning 'well' or 'peacefully'. Sometimes a word itself takes different forms depending on the style. In this case, 잘 is a plain form and 안녕히 is an honorific form (see 2.4 for detail).

2 The verb involved in all styles is 가다 'to go.'
Both the polite-formal style and the polite-informal style(1 & 2) include the honorific marker '시' in the verb while the plain-informal style and the plain style(3 & 4) do not.

All four styles above express a farewell 'Bye' (The literal translation is 'Go in peace'). The polite-formal and the polite-informal styles are used almost interchangeably, without losing politeness. While the polite-formal style is used in formal settings, the polite-informal style is used informally. Either style is perfectly all right to strangers or people you do not know very well. The formal style is most common in written language, while the informal style is used in spoken language. The plain-informal style and the plain style are generally used with colleagues or people who are younger than you are. The plain style is used among close friends and to children.

Knowing the right style of speech is a very complicated matter, which requires more than the grammar of Korean. Let a keen observation and trial-and-error guide you. And until you feel comfortable with the Korean language, it would be a good tactic to use only polite styles.

2.2 THE INFORMAL STYLE

As far as the verb ending is concerned, there are three styles available :
the formal style, the informal style, and the plain style.

Among the 4 styles of speech, the informal style is what you are likely to hear most often. Though it is intimate, it is not rude or does not totally lack politeness. This style is usually used between acquaintances, colleagues, and friends. It is also acceptable with younger people. You can not go wrong with this style.

> **NOTES**
> 1 The formal style has two variants (-습니다, -ㅂ니다)as in 읽습니다, 갑니다.
> 2 The plain style has three variants (-여, -아, -어)as in 사랑해, 살아, 먹어.

The informal style has three variants (-여요, -아요, -어요). The proper ending is added to a verb stem.

1) If the verb stem ends with 하, add -여요.
   Then shorten it (하 + 여요) to 해요.

	Stem – Ending	Contraction
말하다	말하 – 여요	말해요
사랑하다	사랑하 – 여요	사랑해요
운전하다	운전하 – 여요	운전해요

2) If the vowel of the final syllable of a verb stem is either ㅏ or ㅗ, add -아요. Sometimes you need to take a further step to check for possible contraction.

	Stem – Ending	Contraction
살다	살 – 아요	
가다	가 – 아요	가요 (ㅏ+ㅏ→ㅏ)
보다	보 – 아요	봐요 (ㅗ+ㅏ→ㅘ)

3) Otherwise, add −어요. Then check for contraction.

	Stem − Ending	Contraction
읽다	읽 − 어요	
기다리다	기다리 − 어요	기다려요 (ㅣ + ㅓ → ㅕ)
주다	주 − 어요	줘요 (ㅜ + ㅓ → ㅝ)

Exercise : Say the following verbs in informal style.

1 사다 — to buy

2 가르치다 — to teach

3 좋아하다 — to like

4 알다 — to know

5 마시다 — to drink

6 만나다 — to meet

7 배우다 — to learn

8 오다 — to come

Answers

1 사요   2 가르쳐요   3 좋아해요   4 배워요

5 마셔요   6 만나요   7 배워요   8 와요

2.3 MARKERS

In Korean the grammatical functions in a sentence, such as subjects or objects, are determined by the particles that are attached to.

Subjects	Objects	Verbs	
1) 철수가	공을	쳤어요.	Cholsu hit a ball.
2) 공이	철수를	쳤어요.	A ball hit Cholsu.

Examples (1) and (2) use the same words with the exception of particles (underlined). (The basic word order of Korean is that of Subject-Object-Verb.) However, the direction a ball is taking is opposite : In (1), a ball is going from Cholsu, but in (2), a ball is going toward Cholsu. In other words, Cholsu is the actor/doer in (1), but a ball plays that role in (2). The reason for this is not by the word order, but by the particles : 가/이 are subject markers and 을/를 are object markers.

2.3.1 Subject Markers 가/이

1) 철수가 울어요.	Cholsu is crying.
2) 교실이 따뜻해요.	The classroom is warm.

NOTES
1 –가 is used after a word ending in a vowel.
   –이 is used after a word ending in a consonant.
2 These markers can not stand alone.

2.3.2 Object Markers 를/을

1) 나는 김치를 좋아해요.	I like *kimch'i*.
2) 나는 한국말을 공부해요.	I am studying Korean.

NOTES
1 –를 is used after a word ending in a vowel.
   –을 is used after a word ending in a consonant.

2 –은/–는 is used as a subject marker when the subject is not focused.
   –는 is used after a word ending in a vowel.
   –은 is used after a word ending in a consonant.

2.3.3 Other Markers

1) 에
   Point in time   여덟시에 일어나요.
   Location   경남대학교는 마산에 있어요.
   Destination   서울에 가요.

2) 에서
   Place of actions   학교에서 공부해요.
   Place of origin   미국에서 왔어요.

3) 로/으로
   Means of transportation   택시로 가요.
   Means, tools   젓가락으로 먹어요.
   Direction   왼쪽으로 가세요.

Exercise 1 : Fill in the blanks with appropriate markers.
1 나는 당신 ____ 사랑해요.   I love you.
2 날씨 ____ 좋아요.   The weather is nice.
3 바람 ____ 불어요.   The wind is blowing (It's breezy).
4 나는 불고기 ____ 좋아해요.   I like *pulgogi*.
5 나는 신문 ____ 봐요.   I read a newspaper.

Exercise 2 : Identify the particles.
1 공항버스로 공항에 갑니다.
2 공항에서 비행기표를 삽니다.
3 휴게실에서 기다립니다.
4 부산에서 세시에 출발합니다.
5 네시에 서울에 도착합니다.

Answers are on page 51.

2.4 HONORIFICS

Honorifics are polite forms of speech which are used to show respect toward the person you are talking to or the person you are talking about. Some honorific forms are totally different from the plain forms.

2.4.1 Honorific Forms

Plain Forms	Honorific Forms	
1) Nouns		
밥	진지	meal
집	댁	residence
말	말씀	speech
나이	연세	age
이름	성함	name
2) Verbs		
먹다	잡수시다, 드시다	to eat
마시다	드시다	to drink
있다	계시다	to be
자다	주무시다	to sleep
말하다	말씀하시다	to say
죽다	돌아가시다	to die

Compare the phrases on both columns : Plain forms are addressed to a young boy Eugene, while honorific forms are addressed to Mr. Kim.

Plain Forms	Honorific Forms	
유진아, 밥 먹어.	김 선생님, 진지 드세요.	It's mealtime.
유진아, 잘 있어.	김 선생님, 안녕히 계세요.	Bye.

2.4.2 Honorific Markers

Honorifics are formed by adding honorific markers.

1) Personal nouns : Add 님 after personal nouns.

선생	선생님	teacher
교수	교수님	professor
박사	박사님	doctor
아버지	*아버님	father
어머니	*어머님	mother
아들	*아드님	son
딸	*따님	daughter

* Some words involve changes in the syllable before -님 is added : dropping of a final consonant or dropping of the final syllable.

2) Verbs : Add 시/으시 to verb stems.

| 가르치다 | 가르치시다 | to teach |
| 읽다 | 읽으시다 | to read |

NOTE

Use –시– after a vowel. Use –으시– after a consonant.

3) Subject markers : Change 이/가 to 께서.

동생이 보냈어요	My younger sibling sent (me) (a letter).
친구가 보냈어요	My friend did.
할머니께서 보내셨어요.	My grandmother did.

NOTES

1   You received a letter. Find out who sent it :
If it is your younger sister/brother or your friend, use –이 or –가 :
If it is your grandmother, use –께서 as its subject marker.
2   Use –이 after a consonant. Use –가 after a vowel.

4) Indirect object markers : Change 에게 / 한테 to 께.

| 동생에게 보냈어요. | I sent (a letter) to my younger sibling. |

친구에게 보냈어요.   I sent it to my friend.
할머니께 보냈어요.   I sent it to my grandmother.

NOTES

1 This time it is you who sent letters.
   If you sent it to your younger sibling or your friend, use –에게 :
   If you sent it to your grandmother, use an honorific marker –께.
2 The plain forms of indirect object markers are interchangeable,
   as in 동생에게, 동생한테

2.4.3 Humble forms

Lowering yourself is another way of showing respect toward others. This can be accomplished by using humble forms for yourself.

Plain Forms	Humble Forms		
1) Nouns			
나	저	I	저는 대학생입니다.
우리	저희	we	저희는 기숙사에서 삽니다.
2) Verbs			
보다	뵙다	to see	또 뵙겠어요.
주다	드리다	to give	선생님께 드렸어요.
묻다	여쭙다	to ask	말씀 좀 여쭙겠습니다.

2.5 ADDRESSING PEOPLE

1) You

A word for 'you' as an addressee can be dropped freely as long as it is understood between the speakers. The word 선생님 ('a teacher' literally) is most widely used as a neutral and general term for someone not very close even when the addressee is not engaged in teaching profession.

2) Titles

It is best to address people with their titles, for example, 총장 (a university president), 사장(a company president), 박사 (a doctor), or 교수 (a professor). The suffix 님 is added to show respect : Addressing in 선생님 is more polite than 선생. It is a general practice to use last names with titles, such as 임 사장님, 이 교수님, 강 박사님.

3) Family Terms

The Korean language is very rich in family terms : The older the person, the more refined the term. This seems to have come from the tradition that the old are respected. English words 'brother' and 'sister' are not as refined as the Korean counterparts. When you hear 'I have one brother,' age (older or younger in relation to the speaker) or sex (of the speaker) is not known. On the other hand, when its Korean equivalent 형 or 오빠 is mentioned, a definite relationship is revealed. When you have an older brother, you call him 형 if you are male and 오빠 if you are female ; an older sister of a male is called 누나 and an older sister of a female is called 언니. Younger siblings, however, are called 동생 regardless of the speaker's sex. For specification of the sex, 남 (male) or 여 (female) is used, as in 남동생 (younger brother) or 여동생 (younger sister).

Within the family, first names are used only to the younger ones. Suppose 순이 and 분이 are sisters and 순이 is two years older than 분이. 분이 calls her older sister 순이 언니 or 언니, but 순이 calls her younger sister 분이야.

A Korean wife does not take her husband's name when she gets married. A Mr. Kim's wife is called 김선생님 사모님. If she is a mother whose child's name is 순이, then she is called 순이 엄마 (Suni's mother). Between husband and wife, one calls the other 여보, which means 'honey' or 'darling'.

4) Others

A young lady is addressed with -양 after her last name（김양）or after her full name（김순이양）, and a young man with -군（박군）. The adult form of both -양 and -군 is -씨, such as 김순이씨. When a full name is used, the family name is put first and then the given name. Most family names have one syllable（김, 이, 박, 최, 정）, but there are a few exceptions（황보, 선우）. Most given names have two syllables.

When you address shopkeepers, use 아저씨 for male and 아줌마 (shortened from 아주머니) for female. Address unmarried female with 아가씨 instead of 아줌마 since 아줌마 is a term used for married women. The term 아저씨 originally is a family term, meaning 'an uncle'. However, when it is used for someone not related with the speaker, it gives the feeling of closeness.

Exercise : Address properly.

1 Greet the owner of a supermarket as you enter.
2 You ran into your professor on the street.
3 Look for your one and only elder brother at home.
4 A man asks his date（김순이）out for the second time.
5 You ask directions to a saleslady who looks in her late teens.

2.6 NUMBERS

There are two sets of numbers in use : pure Korean numbers and Chinese-derived numbers. Korean numbers are used mostly for counting, while Chinese numbers are used for reading the numerals. However, for the numbers one hundred and above, Chinese numbers are used.

2.6.1 Korean Numbers

1	하나	11	열하나	10	열
2	둘	12	열둘	20	스물
3	셋	13	열셋	30	서른
4	넷	14	열넷	40	마흔
5	다섯	15	열다섯	50	쉰
6	여섯	16	열여섯	60	예순
7	일곱	17	열일곱	70	일흔
8	여덟	18	열여덟	80	여든
9	아홉	19	열아홉	90	아흔
10	열	20	스물		

What makes counting more complicated is that things need specific classifiers (or units). For example, when you count books, the classifier 권 is used as in 책 다섯 권. The trouble is to know which item goes with which classifier. Here are some examples :

	Items	Classifiers	Examples	
1	age	살	(나이)	한 살
2	o'clock (point)	시	(시각)	두 시
3	hours (duration)	시간	(시간)	세 시간
4	people	사람/명, 분	(손님)	네 사람/네 명, 네 분
5	things (general)	개	(의자)	다섯 개
6	animals	마리	(개)	여섯 마리
7	books	권	(책)	일곱 권

8	cars	대	(차)	여덟 대
9	sheets (of paper)	장	(종이)	아홉 장
10	bottles	병	(소주)	열 병
11	cups	잔	(물)	열한 잔
12	pens, pencils	자루	(연필)	열두 자루
13	shoes, socks	켤레	(양말)	열세 켤레
14	a suit of clothes	벌	(양복)	열네 벌
15	trees	그루	(나무)	열다섯 그루

NOTES

1 Any number the last digit of which is 1, 2, 3, or 4 (1, 2, 3, 4, 11, 12, 13, 14, etc.) change their forms when they are followed by classifiers :

하나	→	한	한 잔
둘	→	두	두 시
셋	→	세	세 시간
넷	→	네	네 사람

2 The same is true with the number 20. Compare 20 and 21 :

스물	→	스무 살
스물 하나	→	스물 한 살

2.6.2 Chinese Numbers

1	일	11	십일	10	십	100	백
2	이	12	십이	20	이십	1,000	천
3	삼	13	십삼	30	삼십	10,000	만
4	사	14	십사	40	사십		
5	오	15	십오	50	오십		
6	육	16	십육	60	육십		
7	칠	17	십칠	70	칠십		
8	팔	18	십팔	80	팔십		
9	구	19	십구	90	구십		
10	십	20	이십				

Chinese numbers are used in expressing the following :

1) years	년	천 구백 구십 사년	(1994년)
2) months	월	십이월	(12월)
3) days(of the month)	일	삼십일일	(31일)
4) minutes	분	오십분	(50분)
5) currency : Korean	원	만원	(10,000원)
currency : American	불, 전	십불 구십구전	($ 10.99)
6) floors	층	삼층	(3층)
7) buildings units	동	십사동	(14동)
8) room numbers	호	천백일호	(1101호)
9) telephone numbers	국, 번	사십구국(에) 이천십오번	(49-2015)
		사구(에) 이공일오	

NOTES

1 For telephone numbers, you can read the first set of number/s (neighborhood codes) and the second set (numbers) separately or read each number separately. These two sets of numbers are separated by the word 의 (에 for pronunciation for ease), which here indicates the extention thereof.

2 The word for zero is 공

Months of the Year

1	January	일월		7	July	칠월
2	February	이월		8	August	팔월
3	March	삼월		9	September	구월
4	April	사월		10	October	*시월
5	May	오월		11	November	십일월
6	June	*유월		12	December	십이월

* The names of 6th and 10th month are exceptions : The final consonant is dropped.

Exercise : What do you say?

1 twelve people
2 twenty years old
3 eighteen books
4 one car
5 five hundred sheets of paper

6 August 15
7 October 9
8 12:00
9 4:56
10 3:30

2.7 INTERROGATIVES

1)	<u>누구</u>세요?	<u>Who</u> is it? (to someone at the door)
2)	이름이 <u>무엇</u>이에요?	<u>What</u> is your name?
3)	생일이 <u>언제</u>예요?	<u>When</u> is your birthday?
4)	집이 <u>어디</u>예요?	<u>Where</u> is your house?
5)	<u>왜</u> 울어요?	<u>Why</u> are you crying?
6)	<u>어떻게</u> 지내세요?	<u>How</u> are you doing?
7)	<u>얼마</u>예요?	<u>How much</u> is it?
8)	아이들이 <u>몇</u>이에요?	<u>How many</u> children do you have?
	<u>몇</u>살이에요?	<u>How old</u> are you?
	<u>며칠</u>이에요?	<u>What day</u> (of the month) is it?
9)	<u>무슨</u> 요일이에요?	<u>What day</u> (of the week) is it?
10)	<u>어느</u> 식당에 갈까요?	<u>Which</u> restaurant shall we go to?
11)	<u>어떤</u> 음식을 좋아해요?	<u>What kind</u> of food do you like?

NOTHING PERSONAL   Name the question most frequently asked by Koreans. How old are you's? You got it right. You think Koreans are a very impolite people, asking this personal question the minute they meet you. Just the opposite. They ask this question to be polite. The questioners want to know where exactly they stand agewise since age plays an important role in establishing a speaker-listener relationship in the culture where people respect the old. Remember, nothing personal, not to offend you, but to decide which style of speech to use. Make sense?

2.8 AFFIRMATIVES AND NEGATIVES

Depending on the type of verbs used, negatives are formed differently.

1) 이다 → (이/가) 아니다
   한국사람이에요?   네, 한국사람이에요.   아니오, 한국사람(이) 아니예요.

2) 있다 → 없다
   한국친구 있어요?   네, 있어요.   아니오, 없어요.

3) Other verbs
● Short form : Add 안 before the verb.

   김치(를) 먹어요?   네, 먹어요.   아니오, 안 먹어요.
   차요?   네, 차요.   아니오, 안 차요.
   일해요?   네, 일해요.   아니오, 일 안 해요.

   NOTES
   1 For -하다 verbs, add 안 immediately before -하다.
   2 When you are speaking to close friends or children, you can use 응 for 네 and 아니
     for 아니오. You can also drop the final ending -요.

   네, 있어요.   아니오, 없어요.
   응, 있어.   아니, 없어.

● Long form : Add -지 않 after the verb stem.

   김치(를)먹어요?   네, 먹어요.   아니오, 먹지 않아요.
   차요?   네, 차요.   아니오, 차지 않아요.
   일해요?   네, 일해요.   아니오, 일하지 않아요.

Exercise : Provide negative answers.
1 한국돈 있어요?
2 한국말 공부해요?
3 집에 가요?
4 더워요?
5 동생 있어요?

* Answers are on page 61.

2.9 PAST TENSE MARKERS

Different tenses are formed by adding proper tense markers after the verb stem. Past tense markers have three variants : -였-, -았-, -었-. The last syllable of the verb stem needs to be examined in order to decide on the choice (see 2.2 for comparison). The -어요 ending (the informal style) is used for your practice.

1) If the verb stem ends with 하, add -였-.

	Stem – 였 – Ending	Contraction	
공부하다	공부하 – 였 – 어요	공부했어요	to study
좋아하다	좋아하 – 였 – 어요	좋아했어요	to like
일하다	일하 – 였 – 어요	일했어요	to work
말하다	말하 – 였 – 어요	말했어요	to say

2) If the vowel of the final syllable of a verb stem is either ㅏ or ㅗ, add -았-.

	Stem – 았 – Ending	Contraction	
살다	살 – 았 – 어요	—	to live
가다	가 – 았 – 어요	갔어요	to go
보다	보 – 았 – 어요	봤어요	to see
타다	타 – 았 – 어요	탔어요	to get on

3) Otherwise, add -었-.

	Stem – 었 – Ending	Contraction	
먹다	먹 – 었 – 어요	—	to eat
배우다	배우 – 었 – 어요	배웠어요	to learn
싸우다	싸우 – 었 – 어요	싸웠어요	to fight
가르치다	가르치 – 었 – 어요	가르쳤어요	to teach

Exercise : Transform the following into the past tense, using the –어요 form.

1 전화하다 — to phone
2 오다 — to come
3 기다리다 — to wait
4 만나다 — to meet
5 사다 — to buy
6 읽다 — to read
7 앉다 — to sit
8 입다 — to wear

USEFUL EXPRESSIONS 3

3.1 GREETINGS

DIALOG 1 The Polite-Informal Style

가: 안녕하세요?   How are you?
  Annyŏnghaseyo?
  오랜만이에요.   Long time no see.
  Oraenmanieyo.
나: 네, 안녕하세요?   Fine, how are you?
  Ne, annyŏnghaseyo?
가: 어떻게 지내세요?   How are you doing?
  Ŏttŏk'e chinaeseyo?
나: 잘 지내요.   I'm doing fine.
  Chal chinaeyo.
    ⋮
가: 안녕히 가세요.   Bye.
  Annyŏnghi kaseyo.
  또 뵙겠어요.   See you again.
  Tto poepkkessŏyo.
나: 네, 안녕히 계세요.   Bye.
  Ne, annyŏnghi kyeseyo.

DIALOG 2 The Polite-Formal Style

가: 안녕하십니까?   How are you?
  Annyŏnghashimnikka?
  오랜만입니다.   Long time no see.
  Oraenmanimnida.
나: 네, 안녕하십니까?   Fine, how are you?
  Ne, annyŏnghashimnikka?
가: 어떻게 지내십니까?   How are you doing?
  Ŏttŏk'e chinaeshimnikka?
나: 잘 지냅니다.   I'm doing fine.
  Chal chinaemnida.
    ⋮

가. 안녕히 가십시오.   Bye.
   Annyŏnghi kashipshio.
   또 뵙겠습니다.   See you again.
   Tto poepkkessŭmnida.
나: 네, 안녕히 계십시오.   Bye.
   Ne, annyŏnghi kyeshipshio.

NOTES

1 Dialog 1 is in the polite-informal style. Since this style is used most widely in a casual conversation, the expressions in this book will take this form. Compare this with Dialog 2, which contains the same contents, but in the polite-formal style.

2 The Korean equivalents for 'Bye' have two phrases depending on the direction it is addressed to : 'Bye' to the person who is leaving is 안녕히 가세요 ; 'Bye' to the person who is staying is 안녕히 계세요. When you run into someone on the street, both of you say 안녕히 가세요 to each other because no one is staying. On the other hand, you say 안녕히 계세요 to the person you talked to on the telephone and the response from the other party is also 안녕히 계세요.

Fixed Expressions

감사합니다/고맙습니다.   Thank you.
Kamsahamnida/Komapssŭmnida.

천만에요.   You're welcome.
Ch' ŏnmaneyo.

죄송합니다/미안합니다.   Sorry.
Choesonghamnida/Mianhamnida.

괜찮아요.   That's all right.
Kwaench'anayo.

실례합니다.   Excuse me.
Shillyehamnida.

NOTES

1 Both 감사합니다 and 고맙습니다 express thanks.   감사합니다 is of Chinese origin and 고맙습니다 is pure Korean.
2 The same is true with the phrases for apology,   죄송합니다(Chinese) and 미안합니다 (Korean). However, the expressions of Chinese origin are considered more formal.

Exercise 1 : What's the expression?

1 Long time no see.
2 You are about to hang up the phone. Say 'bye'.
3 How are you doing?
4 I'm doing fine.
5 See you again.

Exercise 2 : Respond appropriately.

1 안녕하세요?   2 어떻게 지내세요?   3 감사합니다.

4 미안합니다.   5 안녕히 가세요.

Answers 1	1 오랜만이에요.	2 안녕히 계세요.	3 어떻게 지내세요?
	4 잘 지내요.	5 또 뵙겠어요.	
Answers 2	1 네 안녕하세요?	2 잘 지내요.	3 천만에요.
	4 괜찮아요	5 안녕히 계세요.	

3.2 INTRODUCING YOURSELF

DIALOG

가: 김 매리입니다.
   Kim Mary imnida.

   처음 뵙겠습니다.
   Ch'ŏŭm poepkkessŭmnida.

나: 이 유진입니다.
   Lee Eugene imnida.

   만나서 반갑습니다.
   Mannasŏ pangapssŭmnida.

I'm Mary Kim.

How do you do?

I'm Eugene Lee.

Glad to meet you.

NOTES

1 Koreans say family name (성) first and then given names (이름).

Family name	Given name	입니다
김	매리	입니다
이	유진	입니다.

2 처음 뵙겠습니다 is an expression used when you meet a person for the first time.

Fixed Expressions

말씀 많이 들었습니다.   I've heard a lot about you.
Malssŭm mani tŭrŏssŭmnida.

잘 부탁합니다.   I hope we can get along well.
Chal put'ak'amnida.

Introduction

안녕하세요.   Hi.
제 이름은 이 유진이에요.   My name is Eugene Lee.
워싱턴에서 왔어요.   I'm from Washington.
존스 홉킨스 대학교에 다녀요.   I go to Johns Hopkins University.
전공은 의학이에요.   My major is medicine.

3.3 AT A DINNER TABLE

DIALOG

(Before the meal)

주인: 어서 드세요.
Host: Ŏsŏ tŭseyo.

손님: 잘 먹겠습니다.
Guest: Chal mŏkkessŭmnida.

Please help yourself.

Thank you, I will.

(During the meal)

주인: 많이 드세요.
Mani tŭseyo.

손님: 불고기가 맛있어요.
Pulgogiga mashissŏyo.

주인: 더 드세요.
Tŏ tŭseyo.

손님: 아니오, 괜찮아요.
Anio, kwaench'anayo.

많이 먹었어요.
Mani mŏgŏssŏyo.

Please have plenty of food.

Pulgogi is delicious.

Please have some more.

No, thank you.

I've had plenty.

(After the meal)

주인: 많이 드셨어요?
Mani tŭshyŏssŏyo?

손님: 네, 잘 먹었습니다.
Ne, chal mŏgŏssŭmnida.

Did you enjoy the food?

Yes, thank you.

NOTES

1 The infinitive for 드세요 is 드시다, which is an honorific form of 먹다 'to eat.'
2 The host or hostess offers food with 드세요, but the guest responds with 먹겠습니다 or 먹었습니다. One does not use honorific forms for oneself.
3 겠 is a future tense marker and 었 is a past tense marker.

Practice

1) When you thank the host for food :

잘 먹겠습니다.   Thanks for the food and I will enjoy it.
잘 먹었습니다.   Thanks for the food and I enjoyed it.

2) When you talk about food :

된장찌개가 뜨거워요.   The pot stew is hot (sense of touch).
불고기가   맛있어요.   *Pulgogi* is delicious.
김치가   매워요.   *Kimch'i* is hot (spicy).

3) When you (as a host) offer food :

아침/점심/저녁 드세요.   Have breakfast/lunch/dinner.
어서   드세요.   Help yourself. (Please go ahead.)
많이   드세요.   Have plenty of food.
맛있게   드세요.   I hope you will find the food delicious.
더   드세요.   Have some more.

4) When you are asked to have more food :

네, 더 주세요.   Yes, please. ('Give me more' literally)
아니오, 괜찮아요.   No, thank you.

Korean Seasonings		Taste
간장	soybean sauce	짜다 (salty)
된장	soybean paste	짜다
고추장	red pepper paste	맵다 (hot in spice)
고춧가루	red pepper powder	맵다
마늘	garlic	맵다
생강	ginger	맵다
깨	sesame	고소하다 (sesame)
참기름	sesame oil	고소하다

Dining Etiquettes

1) Do not hold a spoon and chopsticks together ; Use one thing at a time.
2) It is considered impolite to blow one's nose at a dinner table.

3.4   AT A RESTAURANT (DINING OUT)

DIALOG

가: 뭘 드시겠어요?   What would you like to have?
   Mwol tŭshigessŏyo?
나: 차림표 좀 보여 주세요.   I'd like to see the menu, please.
   Ch'arimp'yo chom poyŏ chuseyo.

(After reviewing the menu)

가: 주문하시겠어요?   Are you ready to order?
   Chumun hashigessŏyo?
나: 네, 냉면 둘 주세요.   Yes, we'll have two *naengmyŏn.*
   Ne, naengmyŏn tul chuseyo.

Practice

1) Making requests
   차림표 좀 주세요.   I'd like to see the menu.
   물수건 좀 주세요.   I'd like to have a wet towel.
   물   좀 주세요.   I'd like to have water.

NOTES

1 좀 functions as a softener when you make requests. The phrases with 좀 are more polite than those without.

2 If you want more of what you have, add 더 after the object.

김치 더 주세요.	I'd like more *kimch'i.*
고추장 더 주세요.	I'd like more red pepper paste.

2) Ordering food

비빔밥	둘	주세요.	I'd like two *pibimbap.*
냉면	두 그릇	주세요.	I'd like two *naengmyŏn.*
불고기	이인분	주세요.	I'd likc two scrvings of *pulgogi.*
맥주	두 병	주세요.	I'd like two bottles of beer.
커피	두 잔	주세요.	I'd like two cups of coffee.

3) Understanding what you hear

주문하시겠어요?	Are you ready to order?
뭘 주문하시겠어요?	What would you like to order?
주문하셨어요?	Have you already ordered?
다 드셨어요?	Are you finished?

4) Korean dishes

김치 *(kimch'i)*: pickles made of cabbage seasoned with red pepper, garlic and many other seasonings

된장찌개 *(toenjang tchigae)*: a pot stew with bean paste as its main ingredient

불고기 *(pulgogi)*: marinated beef

갈비 *(kalbi)*: marinated spare ribs

비빔밥 *(pibimbap)*: rice with assorted mixtures (served hot or cold)

냉면 *(naengmyŏn)*: cold noodles (served with soup, *mul naengmyŏn,* or without soup, *pibim naengmyŏn*)

3·5 AT A COCKTAIL BAR

DIALOG 1

가: 뭘 드릴까요?
　　Mwol tŭrilkkayo?

What would you like to drink?

나: 마가리타 있어요?
　　Margarita issŏyo?

Do you have margarita?

가: 죄송합니다. 없는데요.
　　Choesonghamnida, ŏmnŭndeyo.

Sorry, we don't.

나: 그럼, 진 토닉 주세요.
　　Kŭrŏm, gin tonic chuseyo.

Then, I'll have gin and tonic.

가: 삼천원 선불입니다.
　　Samch'ŏnwon sŏnburimnida.

It's 3,000 won. Please pay in advance.

NOTES

1 margarita : a cocktail made with tequila and lemon or lime juice, usually served with salt
　encrusted on the rim of the glass
2 gin tonic : a cocktail made with gin and tonic water

Practice

1) Asking availability

맥주　　있어요?　　　　Do you have beer?
포도주 있어요?　　　　Do you have wine?
소주　　있어요?　　　　Do you have distilled liquor?

2) Ordering drinks

맥주　　주세요.　　　　I'll have beer.
스카치 주세요.　　　　I'll have Scotch.
콜라　　주세요.　　　　I'll have cola.

3) Making requests or complaints

맥주가 차지 않아요.　　This beer is not cold.
얼음 넣지 마세요.　　　Don't put ice in it.
맥주 한 병 더 주세요.　I'll have one more bottle of beer.

DIALOG 2

가: 뭘 드시겠습니까?   What would you like to have?
　　Mwol tŭshigessŭmnikka?

나: 맥주 주세요.   I'll have beer.
　　Maekju chuseyo.

가: 뭘로 드시겠습니까?   What kind would you like?
　　Mwollo tŭshigessŭmnikka?

나: 뭐(가) 있어요?   What kinds do you have?
　　Mwo(ga) issŏyo?

가: 오비하고 크라운 있습니다.   We have OB and Crown.
　　OB hago Crown issŭmnida.

나: 오비 주세요.   I'll have OB.
　　OB chuseyo.

NOTES

1 뭘 드시겠습니까?
2 뭘로 드시겠습니까?
3 뭐(가) 있어요?

The three words underlined above contain the interrogative 무엇 'what' and respective particles :

뭘   = 무엇 + 을
뭘로 = 무엇 + 으로
뭐가 = 무엇 + 이 (뭐 + 가)   * 뭐 is a short form of 무엇.

Question 1 asks the general idea of what to drink.
Question 2 asks the preference when there are several kinds available such as the kinds of beer. 1 and 2 can be used interchangeably.
Question 3 asks for the selection on what kinds are available. This is often asked by a customer who does not know the selection of a bar.

3·6 AT A STORE

DIALOG

점원: 어서 오세요.　　　　　　　　　　Come in. (Welcome.)
　　　Ŏsŏ oseyo.

　　　뭘 찾으세요?　　　　　　　　　May I help you?
　　　Mwol ch'ajŭseyo?

손님: 영한사전 있어요?　　　　　　　Do you have English-Korean dictionaries?
　　　Yŏnghansajŏn issŏyo?

점원: 네, 있어요.　　　　　　　　　　Yes, we do.
　　　Ne, issŏyo.

손님: 얼마예요?　　　　　　　　　　How much is it?
　　　Ŏlmayeyo?

점원: 만 이천원이에요.　　　　　　　It's 12,000 won.
　　　Man ich'ŏnwonieyo.

손님: 한 권 주세요　　　　　　　　　I'll take one.
　　　Han kwon chuseyo.

점원: 또 오세요.　　　　　　　　　　Please come again.
　　　Tto oseyo.

손님: 수고하세요.　　　　　　　　　Have a good day. (Thank you.)
　　　Sugohaseyo.

NOTES

1 The literal meaning of 뭘 찾으세요? is 'What are you looking for?' This is the expression that the salespeople use when they offer help.

2 You might hear 도와드릴까요? which is the direct translation of 'May I help you?'

Practice

1) When you want to see what you are looking for :

손님: 보여 주세요.   I'd like to see it (Show it to me).

점원: 여기 있어요.   Here it is.

2) When you want something in particular :

손님: 큰 거 있어요?   Do you have a big one?

점원: 없어요.   No, we don't.

3) When you like it :

점원: 이건 어떠세요?   How do you like this?

손님: 좋아요.   I like it.

4) When you decide to take it :

점원: 마음에 드세요?   Do you like it?

손님: 네, 이거 주세요.   Yes, I'll take this.

NOTES

1 More and more people tend to pronounce 거 for 것 (things in general).

다른 거 있어요?   Do you have another one?

까만 거 있어요?   Do you have a black one?

작은 거 있어요?   Do you have a small one?

싼   거 있어요?   Do you have a cheap one?

2 The same holds true for these demonstratives : 이거 (this), 그거 (it), 저거 (that).

3·7   AT A PHARMACY

가: 뭘 찾으세요?
Mwol ch'ajŭseyo?

May I help you?

나: 감기약 주세요.
Kamgiyak chuseyo.

I need medicine for a cold.

가: 어디가 아프세요?
Ŏdiga ap'ŭseyo?

What's the symptom?

나: 기침을 해요.
Kich'imŭl haeyo.

I'm coughing.

Practice

1) Telling what is wrong with you

머리가 아파요.	I have a headache.
배가 아파요.	I have a stomachache.
목이 아파요.	I have a sore throat.
열이 있어요.	I have a fever.
기침을 해요.	I am coughing.
설사를 해요.	I have diarrhea.
변비예요.	I have constipation.
소화가 안 돼요.	I have indigestion.

2) Asking what you need

진통제 주세요.	I need a pain reliever.
소화제 주세요.	I need medicine for indigestion.
감기약 주세요.	I need medicine for a cold.
지사제 주세요.	I need medicine to stop diarrhea.
반창고 주세요.	I need band-aids.
항생제 주세요.	I need antibiotics.

3) Understanding instructions regarding medicine

하루에 세 번 드세요.	Take three times a day.
식후에 드세요.	Take after the meal.
여섯시간마다 드세요.	Take every six hours.
두 알씩 드세요.	Take two tablets each time.
한 봉지씩 드세요.	Take one pack each time.

Practice : Explain your symptoms

3·8 AT A HOTEL

DIALOG

가: 어서 오십시오.
　　Ŏsŏ oshipshio.

　　예약하셨습니까?
　　Yeyak hashyŏssŭmnikka?

나: 네, 데이비드 존슨입니다.
　　Ne, David Johnson imnida.

가: 하루만 주무십니까?
　　Haruman chumushimnikka?

나: 네, 그렇습니다.
　　Ne, kŭrŏssŭmnida.

가: 편히 쉬십시오.
　　P'yŏnhi shwishipshio.

Hi.

Have you made a reservation?

Yes, I'm David Johnson.

Are you staying only one night?

Yes, I am.

Enjoy your stay.

Practice : Focus on what you say.
1) When a doorbell rings :
　　가: <u>누구세요?</u>
　　나: 룸 서비스입니다.
　　가: <u>들어오세요</u>.

Who is it ?
Room Service.
Come in, please.

2) When you call Room Service :

가: 룸 서비스입니다.   Room Service.
나: 얼음 좀 부탁합니다.   I'd like some ice, please.

NOTE

Requests may take the following forms, meaning 'Bring me...

병따개 좀 갖다 주세요.   I need a bottle opener, please.
옷걸이 좀 갖다 주시겠어요?   I need a hanger, please.

Practice : Focus on what you hear.

1) You are asked how long you are going to stay :

가: 며칠 주무십니까(계십니까)?   How long are you going to stay?
나: 이틀 있을 겁니다.   I'm going to stay for two days.

2) You are asked to fill out the registration form :

가: 이 용지에 기록해 주십시오.   Please fill out this form.
나: 네.   O.K.

3) You are asked to sign your name :

가: 여기에 서명해 주십시오.   Please sign here.
나: 네.   All right.

4) You are asked the room number when you ask for the key :

가: 몇 호십니까?   Your room number, please.
나: 1039호입니다.   It's 1039.

5) You are asked if you have laundry to go :

가: 세탁물 있으세요?   Do you have laundry to go?
나: 없어요.   No.

6) You are asked if you had anything from the refrigerator :

가: 냉장고에서 드신 거 있으세요?   Did you have anything from the refrigerator?
나: 없어요.   No.

3·9 ON THE STREET

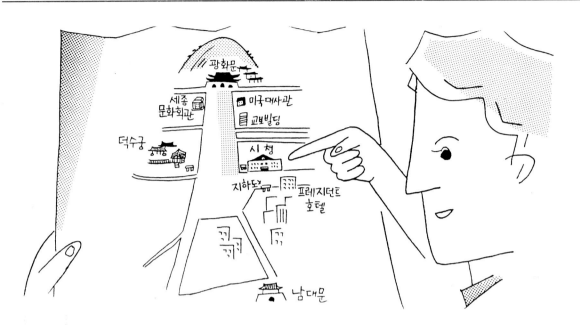

DIALOG

가: 실례합니다.
　　Shillyehamnida.

　　세종문화회관이 어디예요?
　　Sejongmunhwahoegwani ŏdiyeyo?

나: 지하도를 건너세요.
　　Chihadorŭl kŏnnŏseyo.

　　왼쪽에 있습니다.
　　Oentchoge issŭmnida.

가: 감사합니다.
　　Kamsahamnida.

Excuse me.

Where is Sejong Cultural Center?

Cross this underpass.

It's on your left.

Thank you.

Practice

1) When you ask directions to the City Hall:

시청이 어디예요?	Where is the City Hall?
시청이 어디에 있어요?	Where is the City Hall located?
시청이 어느 쪽이에요?	Which way is the City Hall?
시청을 찾는데요.	I'm looking for the City Hall.
시청에 가려면 어떻게 가야 돼요?	How can I get to the City Hall?

2) You are directed to go:

똑바로	가세요.	Go straight.
왼쪽으로	도세요.	Turn left.
오른쪽으로	도세요.	Turn right.

3) You are directed to cross :

길을	건너세요.	Cross the street.
육교를	건너세요.	Cross the overpass.
횡단보도를	건너세요.	Cross the pedestrians' walkway.

4) You are told where the building is :

왼쪽에	있습니다.	It's on your left.
오른쪽에	있습니다.	It's on your right.
가운데에	있습니다.	It's in the middle.
끝에	있습니다.	It's on the corner.

- 시청이 어디예요?
- 오른쪽으로 도세요.

- 경복궁을 찾는데요.
- 길을 건너세요.

- 버스 정류장이 어디에 있어요?
- 똑바로 가세요.

- 서울역은 어느쪽이예요?
- 왼쪽으로 도세요.

- 이태원이 어디예요?
- 지하도를 건너세요.

3·10   ON THE PHONE

DIALOG

가: 여보세요.   Hello.
   Yŏboseyo.
나: 김 선생님 계십니까?   Is Mr. Kim in?
   Kim sŏnsaengnim kyeshimnikka?
가: 접니다.   Speaking.
   Chŏmnida.
나: 안녕하세요, 존 브라운입니다.   Hi, this is John Brown.
   Annyŏnghaseyo, John Brown imnida.

Practice

1) 가: 김 선생님 댁입니까?   Is this Mr. Kim's residence?
   나: 네, 실례지만 누구세요?   Yes, may I ask who's calling?

2) 가: 김 선생님 좀 바꿔 주세요.   May I speak to Mr. Kim?
   나: 잠깐만 기다리세요.   Hold on, please.

3) 가: 김 선생님 계세요?   Is Mr. Kim in?
   나: 안 계세요.   No, he's not.
      방금 나가셨어요.   He has just stepped out.

4) 가: 김 선생님 부탁합니다.   Mr. Kim, please.
   나: 통화중이세요.   He's on another line.

5) 가: 김 순이씨 계십니까?   Is Suni Kim in?
   나: 잘못 거셨어요.   You have the wrong number.
      그런 사람 없어요.   There's no one by that name.

3·11   TRANSPORTATION

3.11.1 Going by Bus

DIALOG

(Getting On 1)

가: 광화문 가요?
   Kwanghwamun kayo?

나: 네, 빨리 타세요.
   Ne, ppalli t'aseyo.

Is this going to Kwanghwamun?

Yes, please hurry up (get on the bus).

(Getting On 2)

가: 한국 대학교(에) 가요?
   Hanguk taehakkyo(e) kayo?

나: 안 갑니다.
   An kamnida.

가: 몇 번 타야 돼요?
   Myŏtpŏn t'aya twaeyo?

나: 20번 타세요.
   Ishipŏn t'aseyo.

Is this going to Hankuk University?

No.

Which bus should I take?

Take No. 20.

(Getting Off 1)

가: 다 왔어요?
   Ta wassŏyo?

나: 네, 여기에서 내리세요.
   Ne, yŏgiesŏ naeriseyo.

Are we almost there?

Yes, get off here.

(Getting Off 2)

가: 어디에서 내려야 돼요?
   Ŏdiesŏ naeryŏya twaeyo?

나: 시청에서 내리세요.
   Shich'ŏngesŏ naeriseyo.

Where should I get off?

Get off at City Hall.

(Getting Off 3)

가: 시청까지 몇 정거장 가야 돼요?
   Shich'ŏngkkaji myŏt chŏnggŏjang kaya twaeyo?

나: 두 정거장 더 가세요.
   Tu chŏnggŏjang tŏ kaseyo.

How many more stops to the City Hall?

You have two more stops to go.

Practice

1) Buying tickets
   승차표(토큰) 열개 주세요.   I want ten tickets (tokens).
   직행버스표 한장 주세요.   I want one ticket.

2) Announcements on the bus
   이번 정차할 곳은 고속버스 터미날입니다.
   This stop is the Express Bus Terminal.
   다음 정차할 곳은 서울역입니다.
   Next stop is Seoul Station.

NOTES

1 There are two types of buses which operate within major cities. One is a regular bus 시
내버스, where there are less seats available. There are two doors : one on the front is
for getting on and the other in the middle is for getting off only. You put your bus token
or exact change in the box next to the driver when you get on the bus.

The other type   좌석버스   seats more people and it costs more. Since it makes less stops than a regular bus, it is faster.

At major bus stops there are bus information stands, which tell you which bus (the bus number/s) to take when you push the button right next to the place of your destination (i.e. 서울역, 이태원).

2   There are also airport buses   공항버스   available for those who make connections to and from the airport. They make stops at major hotels, tourist areas, and shopping districts.

3   There are two kinds of buses which operate from one city to another :
     고속버스 "an express bus" and   시외버스 "a cross-country bus"

3.11.2 Going by Taxi

DIALOG

기사: 어디 가세요?   Where to?
Driver : Ŏdi kaseyo?

손님: 한국은행 갑시다.   To the Bank of Korea.
Passenger : Hangugŭnhaeng kapssida.

                  ⋮

기사: 다 왔습니다.   Here we are.
            Ta wassŭmnida.

손님: 요금이 얼마예요?   How much is the fare?

Yogŭmi ŏlmayeyo?

기사: 천 이백원입니다.
It's 1,200 won.

Ch'ŏn ibaegwonimnida.

손님: 잔돈이 없는데요.
I don't have small bills.

Chandoni ŏmnŭndeyo.

기사: 괜찮습니다.
That's all right.

Kwench'anssŭmnida.

거스름돈 여기 있습니다.
Here's your change.

Kŏsŭrŭmtton yŏgi issŭmnida.

Requests

여기에 세워 주세요.
Pull off here, please.

고속버스 터미날에 내려 주세요.
Let me off at the Express Bus Terminal.

좀 천천히 가세요.
Please slow down.

라디오 좀 줄여 주세요.
Please turn down the radio.

NOTES

1 There are medium-sized taxis and deluxe taxis.
Basic rates (기본요금) and additions are different. Deluxe taxis have been added to the means of transportation lately. These are more comfortable, services are greater, and of course the fare is higher. Night rate (할증료, 20% more) is applied between 12:00 midnight and 4:00 a.m.

2 There are also call taxis available when you need one immediately, but these taxis cost much more than the other types.

3.11.3 Going by Subway

DIALOG

가: 몇 호선 타야 돼요?
Which line should I take?

Myŏt hosŏn t'aya twaeyo?

나: 4호선 타세요.
Take Line 4.

Sahosŏn t'aseyo.

가: 몇 정거장 더 가야 돼요?   How many stops do I have left?
   Myŏt chŏnggŏjang tŏ kaya twaeyo?

나: 네 정거장 더 가야 돼요.   You have four more stops to go.
   Ne chŏnggŏjang tŏ kaya twaeyo.

Practice : Announcements on the train

이번 정차역은 서울역 입니다.
This stop is Seoul Station.
내리실 문은 오른쪽/왼쪽 입니다.
Your exit doors will be on the right / left.
출입문을 열겠습니다.
We are ready to open the doors.
손을 조심하여 주시기 바랍니다.
Watch your hands.
다음 정차역은 동래, 동래역입니다.
The next stop is Tongnae, Tongnae Station.
내리실 손님은 미리 준비하여 출입문 쪽으로 나오시기 바랍니다.
Passengers, if you are getting off, please get ready.
곧 수원행 열차가 도착하겠습니다.
The train bound for Suwon will be arriving soon.

Vocabulary

지하철	a subway	승차권 발매기	a ticket machine
지하철역	a subway station	매표소	a ticket office
타는 곳	tracks	정차역	a train stop
나가는 곳	way out	출입문	a door
갈아 타는 곳	transfer	손님	a passenger
승차권	a subway ticket	열차	a train

3.11.4 Going by Plane

DIALOG *Making a plane reservation*

가: 예약을 하고 싶은데요.   I'd like to make a reservation.
    Yeyagŭl hago shipŭndeyo.

나: 언제 어디에 가십니까?   When and where are you going?
    Ŏnje ŏdie kashimnikka?

가: 토요일 세 시 서울 부탁합니다.   Saturday at 3:00 to Seoul, please.
    T'oyoil seshi Seoul put'ak'amnida.

나: 몇 분이세요?   How many persons are going?
    Myŏt puniseyo?

가: 한 사람입니다.   One person.
    Han saramimnida.

나: 성함이 어떻게 되세요?   May I have your name?
    Sŏnghami ŏttŏk'e toeseyo?

가: 박유진입니다.   I'm Eugene Park.
    Park Eugeneimnida.

나: 전화번호 좀 주세요.   Your phone number, please.
    Chŏnhwabŏnho chom chuseyo.

Reservations

1 예약을 하고 싶은데요.   I'd like to make a reservation.
2 예약 확인을 하고 싶은데요.   I'd like to reconfirm my reservation.
3 예약했는데요.   I made a reservation.

READING

4.1 I (나)

나는 대학생입니다.
워싱턴 디씨에 삽니다.
한국사람입니다.
한국말을 모릅니다.
한국말을 배웁니다.

한국말이 어렵습니다.
듣기[1]는 쉽습니다.
말하기는 어렵습니다.
내[2] 발음은 좋지 않습니다.

NOTES
1 듣기 is a nominal form of 듣다.
2 내 is a materialization of 나+의.

Questions
1 나는 어디에 삽니까?
2 나는 어느 나라 사람입니까?
3 나는 무엇을 배웁니까?
4 말하기는 어떻습니까?
5 내 발음은 어떻습니까?

TRANSLATION

I am a college student.
I live in Washington, D. C.
I am Korean.
I do not know the Korean language.
I am learning Korean.

The Korean language is difficult.
It is easy to understand what other people say.
It is difficult to speak.
My pronunciation is not good.

Practice: Introduce your classmates

Answers

1 나는 워싱턴에 삽니다.
2 나는 한국사람입니다.
3 나는 한국말을 배웁니다.
4 말하기는 어렵습니다.
5 내 발음은 좋지 않습니다.

4.2 LETTER (편지)

이 교수님께,

교수님, 안녕하십니까?
저는 잘 지내고 있습니다.
여름방학동안 한국말을
배우고 있습니다.
친척집에서 지내고 있습니다.

날씨가 아주 덥습니다.
친구들[1]과 한국말을 합니다.
매일 한국음식을 먹습니다.
냉면과 불고기를 좋아합니다.

가을학기에 뵙겠습니다.
안녕히 계십시오.

1994년 8월 15일
한우리 올림[2]

NOTES

1 There are no plural markers in Korean which are equivalent to English book<u>s</u> or bus<u>es</u>. The number itself serves as a marker which differentiates singulars from plurals. A general idea of plurals can be expressed by the suffix -들 as in 친구들 (friends).
2 올림 indicates who the letter is from and is used in letters.

Questions
1 저는 어디에 있습니까?
2 어느 계절입니까?
3 날씨가 어떻습니까?
4 누구한테 편지를 씁니까?
5 저는 어떤 음식을 좋아합니까?

TRANSLATION

Dear Professor Lee,

How are you, sir?
I am doing fine.
I am studying Korean this summer.
I stay at my relative's.

The weather is very hot.
I speak Korean with my friends.
I eat Korean food every day.
I like nacngmyŏn and pulgogi.

I will see you in the fall semester.
Bye.

August 15, 1994
from Uri Han

1 저는 한국에 있습니다.   2 여름입니다.
3 날씨가 아주 덥습니다.   4 교수님께 편지를 씁니다.
5 저는 냉면과 불고기를 좋아합니다.

4.3 MY FAMILY (우리 식구)

우리[1] 식구는 여섯입니다.
언니[2]가 둘, 남동생이 하나 있습니다.
부모님은 워싱턴 디씨에서 일하십니다.
큰 언니는 대학교에서 한국말을 가르칩니다.
작은 언니는 병원에서 일합니다.
둘째 언니는 결혼했습니다.
저[3]는 뉴욕 시청에서 일합니다.
남동생은 버지니아에 삽니다.

주중에는 모두 바쁩니다.
주말에는 식구가 모두 모입니다.

NOTES

1 The Korean language is very rich in family terms. When my family is referred to as a group, the possessive form 우리 (our) is used instead of 내 (my).

2 언니 is a female sibling's older sister. The same person is called 누나 by her brother, a male sibling. When one has two older sisters or brothers, 큰 (the older one) and 작은 (the younger one) differentiate one from the other.

3 저 is a humble form of 나 (I). It is considered more polite than 나 when one talks about oneself in the presence of someone older.

Questions

1 우리 식구는 몇 명입니까?
2 저는 몇째입니까?
3 저는 남자입니까, 여자입니까?
4 작은 언니는 어디에서 일합니까?
5 언제 식구가 모두 모입니까?

TRANSLATION

There are six members in my family.
I have two older sisters and one younger brother.
My parents work in Washington, D.C.
My big sister teaches Korean at a university.
My second sister works at a hospital.
This sister is married.
I work at the City Hall in New York.
My brother lives in Virginia.
On weekdays everybody is busy.
On weekends all of us gather together.

Answers

1 우리 식구는 여섯입니다.
2 저는 셋째입니다.
3 저는 여자입니다.
4 작은 언니는 병원에서 일합니다.
5 주말에 식구가 모두 모입니다.

비행기를 타러[1] 공항에 갑니다.
기차를 타러 역에 갑니다.
고속버스를 타러 고속버스 터미날에 갑니다.
지하철을 타러 지하철 역에 갑니다.
시내버스를 타러 버스 정류장에 갑니다.

옷을 사러 옷 가게에 갑니다.
빵을 사러 제과점에 갑니다.
약을 사러 약국에 갑니다.
책을 사러 서점에 갑니다.
장을 보러 시장에 갑니다.

공부를 하러 학교에 갑니다.
영화를 보러 극장에 갑니다.
점심을 먹으러 식당에 갑니다.
병을 고치러 병원에 갑니다.
남자들은 이발하러 이발소에 가고[2], 여자들은 머리하러 미장원에 갑니다.

NOTES

1 -(으)러 is a verbal form which indicates the purpose of an action. This form is used in the non-sentence final position.

2 -고 connects more than two phrases and it indicates that a sentence is not finished.

Questions

1 기차를 타러 어디로 갑니까?
2 제과점에 무엇을 사러 갑니까?
3 책은 어디에서 삽니까?
4 극장에는 무엇을 하러 갑니까?
5 병을 고치러 어디에 갑니까?

TRANSLATION

We go to an airport to catch a plane.
We go to a train station to take a train.
We go to an express bus terminal to take an express bus.
We go to a subway station to take a subway.
We go to a bus stop to take a local bus.

We go to a clothing shop for clothes.
We go to a bakery for bread.
We go to a pharmacy for medicine.
We go to a bookstore for books.
We go to a market for groceries.

We go to school to study.
We go to a movie theater for movies.
We go to a restaurant for lunch.
We go to a hospital to cure sickness.
Men go to a barber shop to get their hair cut and women go to a beauty salon for their hair.

Answers 1 역에 갑니다. 2 빵을 사러 갑니다. 3 서점에서 삽니다. 4 영화를 보러 갑니다. 5 병원에 갑니다.

4.5 KOREA (한국)

한국은 작은 나라입니다.
한국의 인구는 사천
이백만입니다.
한국의 수도는 서울입니다.

지방에는 아홉개 도[1]가
있습니다.
각 지방의 말씨[2]가 다릅니다.
음식도 다릅니다.

봄, 여름, 가을, 겨울이
있습니다.
여름에는 장마철이
있습니다.

한국은 운동화에서
자동차까지
수출합니다.
한국사람들은 열심히 일합니다.

NOTES

1 There are 9 provinces : 경기도, 강원도, 충청북도, 충청남도, 경상북도, 경상남도, 전라북도, 전라남도, 제주도

2 People speak dialects which are different from one province to another. The difference is felt mostly in its tone.

TRANSLATION

Korea is a small country.
The population of Korea is 42 million.
The capital of Korea is Seoul.

There are nine provinces.
People speak different dialects.
Each province boasts of its unique food.

There are four seasons : spring, summer, fall, and winter.
There is a rainy period in the summer.

Korea exports a variety of goods from running shoes to automobiles.
Koreans work hard.

4.6   SIGHTSEEING IN SEOUL   (서울 구경)

서울은 한국의 수도입니다.
교통이 복잡합니다.
사람들이 많습니다.
고층 아파트도 많습니다.
볼 것도 많습니다.

경복궁에 있는 국립박물관에 갑니다.
선물사러 이태원에 갑니다.
산책하러 한강시민공원에 갑니다.
연주를 들으러 세종문화회관에 갑니다.
밤 경치를 보러 육삼(63)빌딩에 올라갑니다.

TRANSLATION

Seoul is the capital of Korea.
There is a lot of traffic in Seoul.
There are lots of people and high-rise apartments.
There is also a lot to see.

I go to Kyŏngbok Palace and the National Museum.
I go to It'aewon for shopping.
I go to the Public Park along the Han River for a walk.
I go to the Sejong Cultural Center for a concert.
I go up to the Observatory in Yuksam Building for a beautiful nightview.

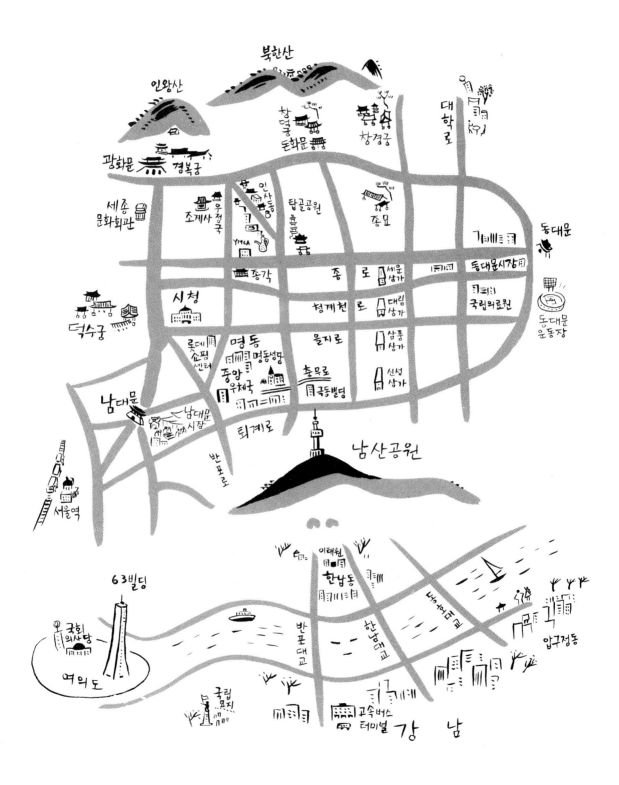

4.7 TRAVELING IN KOREA (한국 여행)

택시를 타고[1] 공항에서 호텔까지 갑니다.
지하철을 타고 서울시내에 갑니다.
케이블 카를 타고 남산[2]에
올라 갑니다.
자동차를 타고 민속촌[3]에 갑니다.
고속버스를 타고 설악산[4]에 갑니다.
기차를 타고 경주[5]에 갑니다.
걸어서 석굴암[6]에 올라 갑니다.
비행기를 타고 제주도[7]에 갑니다.
배를 타고 해금강[8]에 갑니다.

NOTES

1 –를(을) 타고 expresses the means of transportation.

2 남산 (Mt. Namsan) ··· a public park in Seoul, where one can view the whole city of Seoul

3 민속촌 (Korean Folk Village) ··· the open air museum of houses from different provinces, where one can taste traditional Korean food on the spot and one can enjoy traditional performances

4 설악산 (Mt. Sŏrak) ··· a mountain known for its beauty all year round

5 경주 (Kyŏngju) ··· an ancient capital of Shilla Dynasty for 1,000 years, located in Kyongsangbuk-do and one of the major tourist attractions in Korea

6 석굴암 (Sŏkkuram) ··· a cave at a mountain in Kyŏngju, known for its Buddha situated there and the magnificent view at sunrise

7 제주도 (Cheju-do) ··· the biggest island on the south of the peninsula, known for its oranges and the most popular honeymoon resort in Korea

8 해금강 (Haegŭmgang) ··· a scenic canyon of the National Seashore Park in the South Sea off the city of 충무 (Ch'ungmu)

TRANSLATION

We take a taxi from the airport to a hotel.
We take a subway to go downtown Seoul.
We climb Namsan by cable car.
We drive to the Korean Folk Village in Yongin.
We go to Mt. Sŏrak by express bus.
We go to Kyŏngju by train.
We walk to Sŏkkuram.
We fly to Cheju-do.
We go to Haegŭmgang by ship.

4.8 THE KOREAN ALPHABET (한글)

한글은 한국사람의 글입니다.
세종대왕[1]이 만들었습니다.
모든 사람을 위해 만들었습니다.

한글은 배우기가 쉽습니다.
모음 열 개와 자음 열 네 개가 있습니다[2].
미음(ㅁ)글자는 입을 다문 모양과 같습니다.
한글은 아주 과학적입니다.

NOTES

1 세종대왕··· King Sejong, the 4th king of Yi Dynasty (1392-1910)
2 When 한글 was invented, it had 28 letters total. The number of letters presently in use has been
   reduced to 24, with 4 of them out of use.

TRANSLATION

Han'gǔl is the Korean alphabet.
It was invented by King Sejong.
It was made for everybody.

It is easy to learn Han'gǔl.
It has 10 vowels and 14 consonants.
The letter (ㅁ)was made after the shape of closed lips.
Han'gǔl is very scientific.

4.9 KOREAN FOOD (한국 음식)

한국사람은 밥을 먹습니다.
국, 김치와 여러가지 반찬을 먹습니다.
숟가락과 젓가락으로 먹습니다.

불고기와 갈비는 맛있습니다.
수정과와 식혜는 한국 음료입니다.

설날에는 떡국을 먹습니다.
정월 대보름날에는 오곡밥을 먹습니다.
추석날에는 송편을 먹습니다.
동짓날에는 팥죽을 먹습니다.
생일날에는 미역국을 먹습니다.

TRANSLATION

Korean people eat rice.
A meal consists of soup, *kimch'i*, and other side dishes.
They eat with a spoon and chopsticks.

Pulgogi and *kalbi* taste good.
There are traditional Korean drinks; cinnamon drink (수정과) and rice drink (식혜).

Special dishes on special occasions :
Rice cake soup on New Year's Day ;
Rice cooked with five kinds of grain on the 15th of January by the lunar calendar ;
Half-moon shaped rice cake on Korean Thanksgiving (observed August 15 by the lunar calendar)
Red bean porridge on the winter solstice ; and
Seaweed soup on one's birthday.

4.10 KOREAN CUSTOMS (한국 풍습)

한복¹은 한국 고유의 옷입니다.
명절에는 한복을 입습니다.
설날²에는 어른들께 세배를 합니다.
추석³에는 차례를 지냅니다.

방에 들어갈 때 신을 벗습니다.
인사할 때 허리를 굽힙니다.

한국여자는 결혼할 때
남편의 성을 따르지 않습니다.
자식이 부모님을 모십니다.

음식을 여러 번 권합니다.
숫자 4를 싫어합니다.

NOTES

1 한복 (traditional Korean costume) ··· known for its beautiful colors and elegant lines

2 설날 (New Year's Day) ··· a holiday observed by the lunar calendar by most people and bowing to one's elders (세배) that day is a sign of respect, wishing happiness, good health, and a long life.

3 추석 (Korean Thanksgiving) ··· a major holiday observed by the lunar calendar (August 15), which falls on late September or early October. Ceremonies (차례) are held to commemorate the ancestors.

TRANSLATION

Hanbok is a traditional Korean costume.
Koreans wear traditional Korean costumes on holidays.
They bow to elders on New Year's Day.
They hold ceremonies on Thanksgiving.

One takes off one's shoes when one enters a house.
One bows when one greets.

Korean women do not take their husbands' names when they marry.
When parents get old, they are taken care of by their children.

Guests are offered food several times.
Number 4 is avoided.

English-Korean Glossary
for Useful Expressions

		Refer
Are we almost there?	다 왔어요? Ta wassŏyo?	3.11
Are you finished?	다 드셨어요? Ta tŭsyŏssŏyo?	3.4
Are you ready to order?	주문하시겠어요? Chumun hashigessŏyo?	3.4
Bye (to the person who leaves).	안녕히 가세요. Annyŏnghi kaseyo.	3.1
Bye (to the person who stays).	안녕히 계세요. Annyŏnghi kyeseyo.	3.1
Come again.	또 오세요. Tto oseyo.	3.6
Come in.	어서 오세요. Ŏsŏ oseyo.	3.6
Did you enjoy the food?	많이 드셨어요? Mani tŭsyŏssŏyo?	3.3
Do you have beer?	맥주 있어요? Maekju issŏyo?	3.5
Excuse me.	실례합니다. Shillyehamnida.	3.1
Get off here.	여기에서 내리세요. Yŏgiesŏ naeriseyo.	3.11
Glad to meet you.	반갑습니다. Pangapssŭmnida.	3.2
Have more (food).	더 드세요. Tŏ tŭseyo.	3.3
Have plenty of food.	많이 드세요. Mani tŭseyo.	3.3
Hello.	여보세요. Yŏboseyo.	3.10

Help yourself.	어서 드세요. Ŏsŏ tŭseyo.	3.3
Hold on.	잠깐만 기다리세요. Chamkkanman kidariseyo.	3.10
How are you?	안녕하세요. Annyŏnghaseyo.	3.1
How are you doing?	어떻게 지내세요? Ŏttŏk'e chinaeseyo?	3.1
How do you do?	처음 뵙겠습니다. Chŏŭm poepgessŭmnida.	3.2
How many more stops do I have?	몇 정거장 가야 돼요? Myŏt chŏngŏjang kaya twaeyo?	3.11
How many persons are going?	몇 분이세요? Myŏt puniseyo?	3.11
How much is it?	얼마예요? Ŏlma yeyo?	3.6
Hurry up (getting on the bus).	빨리 타세요. Ppalli t'aseyo.	3.11
I am doing fine.	잘 지내요. Chal chinaeyo.	3.1
I enjoyed the food.	잘 먹었습니다. Chal mŏgŏssŭmnida.	3.3
I have had plenty.	많이 먹었어요. Mani mŏgŏssŏyo.	3.3
I have heard a lot about you.	말씀 많이 들었습니다. Malssŭm mani tŭrŏssumnida.	3.2
I hope we can get along well.	잘 부탁합니다. Chal put'ak'amnida.	3.2
Is Mr. Kim in?	김 선생님 계세요? Kim Sŏnsaengnim Kyeseyo?	3.10
Is this bus going to the City Hall?	시청 가요? Shich'ŏng kayo?	3.11
It is delicious.	맛있어요. Mashissŏyo.	3.3

It is hot (sense of touch).	뜨거워요.	3.3
	Ttŭgŏwoyo.	
It is hot (spicy).	매워요.	3.3
	Maewoyo.	
It is on your left.	왼쪽에 있습니다.	3.9
	Oenjjoge issŭmnida.	
I want to make a reservation.	예약을 하고 싶은데요.	3.11
	Yeyagŭl hago ship'ŭndeyo.	
I will enjoy the food.	잘 먹겠습니다.	3.3
	Chal mŏkkessŭmnida.	
I will have *naengmyon*.	냉면 주세요.	3.4
	Naengmyŏn chuseyo.	
I would like more *kimchi*.	김치 더 주세요.	3.4
	Kimch'i tŏ chuseyo.	
I would like some ice.	얼음 좀 부탁합니다.	3.8
	Ŏrŭm chom put'ak'amnida.	
I would like to see the menu.	차림표 좀 보여 주세요.	3.4
	Ch'arimpyo chom poyŏ chuseyo.	
I would like water.	물 좀 주세요.	3.4
	Mul chom chuseyo.	
Long time no see.	오랜만이에요.	3.1
	Oraenmanieyo.	
May I help you?	뭘 찾으세요?	3.6
	Mwŏl ch'ajŭseyo?	
May I speak to Mr. Kim?	김 선생님 좀 바꿔 주세요.	3.10
	Kim sŏnsaengnim chom pakkwo chuseyo.	
Pay in advance.	선불입니다.	3.5
	Sŏnpurimnida.	
Pull over here.	여기에 세워 주세요.	3.11
	Yŏgie sewo chuseyo.	
See you again.	또 뵙겠어요.	3.1
	Tto poepkessŏyo.	
Slow down.	천천히 가세요.	3.11
	Ch'ŏnch'ŏni kaseyo.	

Sorry.	죄송합니다/미안합니다.	3.1
	Choesonghamnida/Mianhamnida.	
Speaking.	접니다.	3.10
	Chŏmnida.	
Thank you.	감사합니다/고맙습니다.	3.1
	Kamsahamnida/Komapsŭmnida.	
Thank you and have a good day.	수고하세요.	3.6
	Sugohaseyo.	
That is all right.	괜찮아요.	3.1
	Kwaench'anayo.	
The line is busy.	통화중이에요.	3.10
	T'onghwajungieyo.	
There is no one by that name.	그런 사람 없어요.	3.10
	Kŭrŏn saram ŏpsŏyo.	
This stop is Pusan Station.	이번 정차역은 부산역입니다.	3.11
	Ibŏn chŏngch'ayŏgŭn pusanyŏgimnida.	
You have the wrong number.	잘못 거셨어요.	3.10
	Chalmot kŏsyŏssŏyo.	
What kinds do you have?	뭐 있어요?	3.5
	Mwŏ issŏyo?	
What is the symptom?	어디가 아프세요?	3.7
	Ŏdiga ap'ŭseyo?	
What would you like to have?	뭘 드시겠어요?	3.4
	Mwol tŭshigessŏyo?	
Where are you going?	어디 가세요?	3.11
	Ŏdi kaseyo?	
Where is the City Hall?	시청이 어디예요?	3.9
	Shich'ŏngi ŏdiyeyo?	
Where should I get off?	어디에서 내려야 돼요?	3.11
	Ŏdiesŏ naeryŏya twaeyo?	
Which bus should I take?	몇 번 타야 돼요?	3.11
	Myot pŏn t'aya twaeyo?	
Which line should I take?	몇 호선 타야 돼요?	3.11
	Myŏt hosŏn t'aya twaeyo?	

Who is calling?	누구세요? Nuguseyo?	3.10
Who is it?	누구세요? Nuguseyo?	3.8
You are welcome.	천만에요. Ch'ŏnmaneyo.	3.1

Word List

ㄱ

ㅅ

ㅇ

ㅋ

ㅌ

ㅍ

ㅎ

Survival Situational Korean

Did you know that you need only a few phrases to accomplish your goal in a certain situation? For example, you go to a Korean restaurant. Your objective there is how to place an order. The focus of your lesson, then, is learning how to order food. The following is a list of expressions you will need according to the situations :

01 Greetings

안녕하세요?	Hi, how are you?
오랜만이에요.	Long time no see.
어떻게 지내세요?	How are you doing?
감사합니다/고맙습니다.	Thank you.
천만에요.	You're welcome.
죄송합니다/미안합니다.	Sorry.
괜찮아요.	That's all right.
실례합니다.	Excuse me.

02 Introducing Yourself

처음 뵙겠습니다.	How do you do?
반갑습니다.	Glad to meet you.
잘 부탁합니다.	I hope we can get along well.

03 At a Dinner Table

잘 먹겠습니다.	I will enjoy the food.
잘 먹었습니다.	I enjoyed the food.
맛있어요.	It is delicious.

04 At a Restaurant

비빔밥 주세요.	I'd like to have pibimbap.
물 좀 더 주세요.	I'd like to have more water.

05 At a Cocktail Bar

콜라 있어요?	Do you have cola?
맥주 주세요.	I'd like to have beer.

06 At a Store

보여 주세요.	I'd like to see it.
큰 거 있어요?	Do you have a big one?
얼마예요?	How much is it?
이거 수세요.	I'll take this.
수고하세요.	Bye (to a shopkeeper).

07 At a Pharmacy

간기야 주세요.	I'd like medicine for a cold.
열이 있어요.	I have a fever.

08 At a Hotel

얼음 좀 부탁합니다.	I'd like to have ice, please.
누구세요?	Who is it?

09 On the Street

시청이 어디예요?	Where is the City Hall?
시청을 찾는데요.	I'm looking for the City Hall.

10 On the Phone

여보세요.	Hello.
김 선생님 계세요?	Is Mr. Kim in?
김 선생님 좀 바꿔 주세요.	I'd like to speak to Mr. Kim, please.

11 By Bus

시청 가요?	Is this going to the City Hall?
몇 번 타야 돼요?	Which bus should I take?

다 왔어요?   Are we almost there?
어디에서 내려야 돼요?   Where should I get off?

12 By Taxi

김포공항 갑시다.   Let's go to Kimpo Airport.
여기에서 세워 주세요.   Pull over here, please.

13 By Subway

몇 호선을 타야 돼요?   Which line should I take?
몇 정거장 더 가야 돼요?   How many more stops do I have left ?

14 By Plane

예약을 하고 싶은데요.   I'd like to make a reservation.
서울행 세시 반 부탁합니다.   I'm going to Seoul at 3:30, please.